Pray FOR YOUR Friends

THE 8 PRAYERS OF JOB

*An Ancient Antidote
to Today's Polarized World*

JOE TYE

A RADICAL NEW UNDERSTANDING OF
THE OLDEST BOOK IN THE BIBLE

Cover art: From *Illustrations of the Book of Job* by William Blake (1826)

Design by Studio 6 Sense | studio6sense.com

www.PrayForYourFriends.com

ISBN 13: 978-1-887511-53-7
ISBN 10: 1-887511-53-9

For Mom who, whatever challenges she herself
was facing, has always made a priority
of praying for her friends.

Contents

"The function of prayer is not to influence God, but rather to change the nature of the one who prays."

Soren Kierkegaard

"After Job had prayed for his friends, the Lord made him prosperous again and gave him twice as much as he had before."

Job 42:10

INTRODUCTION

If there was a prayer that could help you build strength of character, cultivate spiritual peace, foster more loving and lasting relationships, and achieve goals, dreams, and a quality of life that might today seem impossible, would you pray it? And if you knew that prayer would help to heal our polarized world, wouldn't you want to be part of a movement to encourage others to pray it?

In the Book of Job, we are given such a prayer. "Pray for your friends" is a command that conveys far more than a simple reading of those words might seem to imply. When God told Job, toward the end of the story that bears his name, to pray for his friends, He was doing much more than instructing Job to say the words. He was telling him to melt the ice that had, following the series of horrible tragedies that Satan had inflicted upon him, frozen his soul. We do not, and cannot, know the precise words Job spoke, but the Bible tells us that God listened to Job's prayer, and that it was *after* he said the words that Job's life was transformed. The ultimate beneficiaries of Job's prayer were not the friends he had prayed for – the real beneficiary was Job himself. The eight prayers that are implicit in Job's act of praying for his friends can change your life as well. These eight prayers, were we all to pray them, could change our world.

Now, before you go racing off for your Bible to look up eight prayers that you don't remember having seen in the Book of Job, I'll tell you that you have to read between the lines. In fact, more than reading between the lines, seeing eight different prayers packed into the four words "pray for your friends" requires an attempt to read the mind of God, to the extent that a mere mortal can presume to do that. That is why I wrote this book – to share with you what I believe is the central message of this often-misunderstood book. To share with you my understanding of *why* God told Job to pray for his friends.

In the introduction to his essay collection *Dimensions of Job,* Nahum N. Glatzer said that most of the people who have written about Job over the centuries have re-created the book to fit their own images and preconceptions, whether Jewish, Muslim, Christian, humanist, or whatever. I'm no different. I interpret Job through the lens of my work as a writer and speaker on personal values, leadership, and human motivation. In effect, I'm seeing in the Book of Job what I want to see, and what I want you to see. But I also believe the eight powerful prayers that I see in Job's prayer for his friends are what God would want us all to see, whatever our religious belief or non-belief happens to be.

These eight prayers would be a pretty good prescription for heaven on earth, were we all to adopt them. Not a Shangri-La of ease and indulgence, but a kingdom of love and compassion, of liberation from ego and self-centeredness. A place where people really cared for one another. If we humans really are created in the image of God, and if God really is loving and compassionate, then praying for our friends (and continuously expanding the number of people we include in that circle of people we call friends) will help us live up to the image, and the expectations, of God.

These eight prayers would be a pretty good prescription for heaven on earth, were we all to adopt them.

In this book, I refer to God as He because that is how God is portrayed in the Book of Job, not because I believe that God is an old (very old!) man up in the sky. I will also acknowledge that when it comes to answering questions about the true nature of God, my ignorance is every bit as profound as the ignorance of Job; neither of us were there when God laid down the roots of the mountains or fixed the stars in the firmament, much less have a clue as to what God was doing before the Big Bang. But I'm certain that Job, like me, experienced an overwhelming sense of awe and mystery when walking in the mountains and gazing up at the nighttime sky. And I'm also certain that I, like Job before me, can change my life if I, like him, learn to worry less about my own troubles and instead pray for my friends.

TODAY MORE THAN EVER

In the early 21st century our nation is more polarized than it has been for a very long time. Politicians, biased media, and fringe hate groups have weaponized social media, using it as a platform for bullying, threatening and vilifying – using it to transform opponents into enemies. Trust in government, business, healthcare, and religious entities has plummeted. Across the spectrum fear and hatred are being stoked up for personal and political gain. Compromise (a marriage of the words common and promise) is too often seen as a betrayal – as sleeping with the enemy – rather than as a means of finding common ground to achieve goals that benefit everyone, and not just the tribe or the base.

The level of incivility in our society has reached crisis proportions. This is being recognized by thought leaders in many disciplines. In *The Hospitable Leader: Create Environments Where People and Dreams Can Flourish*, church leader Terry Anderson writes: "The very environment around us feels charged with an almost tangible negativity… The polarization of our society is damaging to any effort to achieve anything great." In *Deep Medicine: How Artificial Medicine Can Make Healthcare Human Again,* Dr. Eric Topol writes of "a profound lack of human connection and empathy in medicine today... with disenchanted patients largely disconnected from burned-out, depressed doctors."

And in *Love Your Enemies: How Decent People Can Save America from the Culture of Contempt,* Arthur Brooks, President of the conservative think tank American Enterprise Institute, writes: "Political scientists find that our nation is more polarized than it has been at any time since the Civil War. This is especially true among partisan elites – leaders who, instead of bringing us together, depict our differences in unbridgeable, apocalyptic terms." Brooks distinguishes between anger, which he says can be legitimate and constructively channeled into positive change, and contempt. The latter, he says, is poisoning our culture. To hold a person, or a group of people, in contempt is the antithesis of caring for them. One does not pray for people for whom they harbor contempt.

The lesson of the Good Samaritan, many seem to feel, is for suckers while "looking out for number one" is the rule of the day. Praying for your friends seems quaint and out of touch, while praying for your enemies is seen as naïve and stupid. Today more than ever our world could benefit from a revolutionary reinterpretation of the Book of Job. Today more than ever we are called to pray for our friends – and for those who could become our friends were we to pray for them. Today more than ever we should expect this level of caring of ourselves and each other, and demand it of our leaders.

A BRIEF SYNOPSIS OF
THE BOOK OF JOB

Scholars believe that the Book of Job is the oldest book in the Bible. In the story, Satan (the adversary) wagers God that he can cause Job, a man God calls his most faithful and blame-free servant, to lose his faith. God gives Satan the go-ahead to inflict hideous calamities upon His faithful servant. In one day, Satan causes a windstorm to kill all of Job's ten children, bandits to murder his servants and steal his earthly possessions, and inflicts his body with painful boils. Four of Job's "friends" come to comfort him but in various ways they each end up accusing him of having been an evil man who is now being punished for past wickedness, a charge that Job vehemently denies even as he sinks ever lower into the swamp of depression and self-pity. Finally, God Himself comes out of the whirlwind to confront Job with his ignorance and to chastise his friends for having presumed to speak for God. God then instructs Job to pray for his friends, after which we are told that Job was given a new family, great wealth, and a very long life (another 140 years).

Did all of these things actually happen in the real world, as biblical literalists choose to believe? Or is this a beautifully written metaphor intended to instruct, the way all great teachers, including Jesus, have created metaphors to make complex lessons more easily grasped? I happen to believe the latter, but it does not really matter what you or I believe about the story; the lessons apply just the same.

Bible citations are from the New International Version. Whatever version of the Bible you have on your bookshelf or bedside table, I encourage you to read (or re-read) the Book of Job and see if you don't gain new insights of your own.

Part 1

Transformation

THE REAL
MESSAGE OF JOB

Anyone who utters that inane platitude about "the patience of Job" has obviously not read the Book of Job very carefully. Job was grief-stricken, anguished, angry, hostile, self-pitying, and anything but patient. He had no patience whatsoever for his friends' argument that he must have done something terribly wrong to have deserved the train of tragedies which had, within the course of a single day, killed every one of his ten children, wiped out the wealth he had worked a lifetime to create, and left his body wracked with pain. He mourned the day he was born and wished that he would quickly die. Job accused God of having done wrong by him, and he demanded answers. No, Job was not a patient man.

In a frequently overlooked passage near the end of the book that bears his name, this angry and self-pitying man was instructed by God to pray a particular prayer. He was told to pray for his friends, the men Job had called "miserable comforters" who had all but accused him of bringing a chorus of calamity down on his head through his past transgressions. We are told that God accepted Job's prayer, and subsequently blessed him with a new family, enormous wealth, and long life.

We can never know the specific words that Job used in the prayer for his friends, but we can imagine it must have gone against the grain of every fiber in his heart to say those words. We can guess that he was not being absolutely sincere as he prayed for the "friends" who had tried to blame him for the avalanche of adversity that had darkened his life, and that a little voice in the back of his head was recanting the prayer even as the words were leaving his mouth. His friends, after all, in presuming to be speaking for God, had in fact become advocates for the position of Satan. They had accused Job of having broken faith with God, just as Satan had predicted he would do were he to lose everything that was dear to him.

Nor do we know in what way Job's prayer was granted, or for sure even if it was granted; God said only that he would *accept* Job's prayer, not necessarily that He would honor it. We have no idea what happened to Job's friends once they left his presence. But we do know – and the text is quite clear and specific about this – it was *after* Job had prayed for his friends that his life turned around and he once again became prosperous and content. That is, I believe, the central message of the Book of Job. Bad things do happen to good people; bad things will happen to you in all likelihood. The message of Job is that when bad things do happen, instead of playing the role of the victim and complaining about your problems – the way Job did for much of the book – you should reach out and pray for your friends. Paradoxically, praying for others might well give you the courage and strength you need to deal with your problems more effectively than would praying that God fix those problems for you.

What are you doing when you respond to your trials by praying for your friends? I believe you're really praying eight prayers. You see, when Job prayed for his friends – when any of us stop thinking about our own selves and our problems and pray for someone else – we, like Job, are praying an eightfold prayer, whether we explicitly think of it in those terms or not. We are praying for acceptance, forgiveness, reconciliation, compassion, hope, transcendence, connection, and renewal.

These eight prayers, were we all to pray them, could help to solve almost every problem in our world. At a personal level, these prayers offer a remedy for anxiety, depression, low self-esteem, self-centeredness, and many of the other psychological and emotional problems that are the plague of our era.

In organizations, a culture where managers prayed for the people they managed, and where coworkers saw each other as friends to be prayed for, would attract and retain a high-caliber and highly-dedicated workforce. The eight prayers that I impute to the words "Pray for your friends" are actually a pretty good formula for servant leadership and for building a more positive organizational culture.

At a societal level, these eight prayers are an antidote to the narcissism, mindless self-indulgence, and entitlement mentality that characterize a "looking out for number one" culture. If we expected our political leaders to pray for their constituents instead of seeking to polarize them by turning opponents into enemies, we would have a much more civil discourse. Because politics is the art of the possible, and compromise is what makes those things possible, our leaders would accomplish much more. And at the global level, were these prayers to become universal, they could bring about an end to intolerance, hatred, violence, and indeed war itself.

Theologians tell us that the real purpose of prayer is not to influence God but rather to change the one who prays. In *War and the Soul: Healing our Nation's Veterans from Post-Traumatic Stress Disorder*, Dr. Edward Tick wrote that PTSD is not just a stress disorder; it is also an *identity* disorder. The combat veteran who was once ordered to kill other human beings, and was perhaps injured in the process, who is now thumping cantaloupes in the grocery story, struggles with the question: which one is the real me? The first task for someone who has endured the sort of tragedy that was inflicted upon Job is to restore a sense of who they are and to not allow themselves to be defined by what has happened to them. Perhaps more than anything, the eight prayers described in this book are meant to help the individual who has suffered through adversity to emerge stronger, more resilient, and with a more positive self-identity.

The eight prayers described in this book are meant to help the individual who has suffered through adversity to emerge stronger, more resilient, and with a more positive self-identity.

In the sense that I am using the phrase, "pray for your friends" does not necessarily mean to ask a divine deity to intervene on their behalf. Rather, I mean it in the sense of genuinely caring for that person's welfare and acting in their best interests. It means to have empathy for another human being.

Looking more Deeply into the Book of Job

Before we explore what I define as the eight prayers of Job and their incredible potential to change your life, let's look a little more closely at the Book of Job – what it is and what it is not. Like the story of Adam and Eve being evicted from the Garden of Eden and the Valley of the Shadow of Death in the 23rd Psalm, the story of Job is a powerful metaphor for the inevitability of suffering, and the hope of redemption, in the human experience. According to the *Oxford Companion to the Bible*, Job is also "a work of intellectual vigor" and "a literary masterpiece that belongs with the classics of world literature." Every time I read it, I marvel at the emotional depth and the poetic imagery that are packed into this amazing piece of scripture. But the very brilliance of the poetry tends to overshadow what I believe is the core message, which we do not see until almost the very end of the story.

The traditional interpretation is that the Book of Job is about the nature of human suffering and of finding the courage and strength to endure it. In *Let God Be God: Life-Changing Truths from the Book Job,* Ray C. Stedman wrote: "Our sufferings often seem meaningless, yet there is a lesson for all of us in Job's life and the lives of all those who endure persecution, martyrdom, injury, cancer, multiple sclerosis, poverty, and countless other types of trials. The lesson is that testing purifies us and reveals the gold of proven, refined character within us." And in *Job: A Man of Heroic Endurance,* Charles Swindoll writes that this is the ultimate lesson of the Book of Job: "When trouble comes we have two options. We can view it as an intrusion, an outrage, or we can see it as an opportunity to respond in specific obedience to God's will."

Job certainly did endure catastrophic adversity and survive it, but the traditional view essentially assumes that the book's lesson ends with that – with "the patience of Job." This traditional perspective ignores what I contend is the most important lesson of all, the one captured in these four words: *Pray for your friends.* Job's story does not end when his suffering ended, quite to the contrary. It was really just beginning then. The personal transformation that set the stage for the magnificent second half of Job's life began with him praying for his friends.

At the most fundamental level, I do not believe that the Book of Job is literally the story of a wager between God and Satan, with Satan betting that he could, with God's go-ahead, shatter Job's faith by having his family and his servants slaughtered, his great wealth taken from him, and his body ravaged by disease. Who could believe in, much less worship, a deity who would boast to Satan about his servant Job the way you or I might brag about a well-trained dog, and who would then sanction the murder of that servant's children with no greater remorse than you or I might have about calling an exterminator to rid the basement of termites? And sanction these murders only to prove that this loyal servant would not turn around and bite his master, no matter how badly he'd been abused?

Nor, as is commonly understood, is this the story of how one man's faith was tested by adversity, and how that man survived the test with flying colors. To be sure, Job's faith *was* tested by the sudden deaths of his children and servants and the devastation of his body. And to be sure, while his faith did waver it never broke. But if this really was a test, it was a test that was fatally flawed. In the biblical story, God wins His bet with Satan, but that's only because Job never learns the whole truth – *that it was God Himself* who gave Satan the approval he needed to kill Job's children and deprive him of his health, wealth, and happiness. Had Job been told that God had condoned Satan's crimes in advance, and that it had been within His power to prevent Satan from committing those crimes, who could doubt that his faith would not have been utterly crushed?

Finally, the Book of Job is not the story of how a man was rewarded by God for his enduring faith. For one thing, many scholars believe that the happy ending in which God gives Job long life, a new family, and great wealth is a later addition to the original story (we will revisit this below). More to the point, to believe that God rewarded Job for passing a test of faith the way Santa Claus rewards good little boys and girls at Christmas is to accept the very argument for which God rebuked Job's friends: that through our earthly behavior we can somehow manipulate God's divine behavior.

If Job is not the literal story of a bet between God and Satan, or of how one man survived the test of faith and was rewarded for his faithfulness, what is it about? I believe the entire story revolves around this one key phrase, the way a gyroscope balances on a single fine point, serving as a universal and eternal guide to us all for how to handle ourselves during troubled times. These four words: *Pray for your friends.*

As Harold Kushner eloquently argues in *When Bad Things Happen to Good People* (note that he says *when*, not *if,* bad things happen to good people), the Book of Job is a profound exploration of what Kushner calls the only question that really matters: *why* do bad things happen to good people? Kushner concludes that God does not cause, or even allow (as in a bet with Satan) these bad things to happen. They happen because there is an element of randomness in the universe. They happen because for God to deprive people of the free will to do evil would also deprive us of the free will to do good. Bad things happen, they just do.

That brings us to a corollary question that matters even more: what do we do when bad things happen? W Mitchell is a veteran of bad things happening to good people. As a young man, he was riding his motorcycle through the streets of San Francisco when a truck ran a stop sign and plowed into him. The motorcycle's gas tank exploded, and Mitchell became a human torch; his face and hands were burned off in the inferno. After agonizing years of surgery and rehabilitation, he arduously rebuilt his life. He moved to Colorado, started a business, ran for mayor of his small-town (campaign slogan: "not just another pretty face"), and even learned how to fly an airplane equipped with special controls.

One day Mitchell's plane crashed on takeoff and his back was broken. Now, in addition to being seriously disfigured, he was paralyzed. More agonizing years of rehabilitation followed. Through it all, he developed a personal power that's embodied in the philosophy of his book *It's Not What Happens to You It's What You Do About It.*

What should good people do when bad things happen? The answer is buried deep in the final lines of the Book of Job. It's easy to overlook; most people do overlook it. *Pray for your friends.* Rise above your own personal problems and pray for, and work for, something that is bigger than you. Thinking deeply about Job's prayer can help us all make sense of a world in which bad things happen to good people. More important, it can guide us to the right answer to the question: what should we do when bad things happen to us?

> **Thinking deeply about Job's prayer can help us all make sense of a world in which bad things happen to good people. More important, it can guide us to the right answer to the question: what should we do when bad things happen to us?**

THE TRANSFORMATION OF GOD, AND THE TRANSFORMATION OF JOB

Can you imagine what legendary filmmaker Cecil B. DeMille, the man who depicted Moses parting the Red Sea on the silver screen, would have done with this scene? God in all His glory emerges from the whirlwind to confront poor Job in all his ignorance. *Where were you,* God demands to know, *when I laid down the mountains and corralled the seas? Can you capture and bind the stars or tame the Leviathan, little man?* God's thunderous inquisition must have made the very ground quake: *Who has a claim against me that I must pay? Everything under heaven belongs to me.*

Poor Job quivers and cowers, repenting in dust and ashes. Then God turns his wrath upon Job's friends, for "they have not spoken the truth." Now, can't you just picture these poor wretches groveling in their own turn? Especially when God places their fates squarely in the hands of Job, the man they had only moments before falsely accused of wrongdoing. "My servant Job will pray for you," God says, "and I will accept his prayer and not deal with you according to your folly." We are told that Job did pray for the three men, and that God did accept his prayer.

What are we to make of this sequence? Surely, God needed neither Job's prayer nor his permission to deal with the friends as He saw fit. Alternatively, as Kushner argues, God cannot be directed by our prayers to intervene in human affairs and was under no obligation to listen to, much less honor, whatever Job requested in his prayer. Furthermore, whatever Job might have felt in his heart about whether his friends deserved his prayers, with God towering over him he doubtlessly felt he had no choice but to get down on his knees and at least say the words under duress, praying a prayer that God would have known was a false prayer, a fraud.

There must be something else going on here, something that can only be picked up by thinking more deeply about why God showed Himself to Job, and why he commanded Job to pray for his friends as opposed to, say, commanding Job to grovel in the dust and worship The Lord.

There is.

When God told Job to pray for his friends, He was in effect telling him to get over it, to stop obsessing about his own problems and show concern for the problems of others. We are not told about the specifics of Job's prayer for his friends – whether he prayed for their eternal salvation, that they would win big in the Chaldean lottery, or if it was simply a prayer for safe travels. For all we can tell from reading the story, Job might have prayed that all the bad things which had happened to him would now happen to them, proving his point that just because bad things happen to you doesn't necessarily mean that you are a wicked person who deserves to have those bad things happen.

Nor are we told what God did with Job's prayer, beyond accepting it. Did the three men win big in the Chaldean lottery, or merely make it safely home?

Or did they arrive home to find the aftermath of a bloody massacre like the one that took Job's family? We can never know. But that's not what this story is about.

When God appears from out of the whirlwind, he is overawing, intimidating, even bullying, as if saying to Job, "who are you, little man, to question My purpose and measures?" He is THE LORD, larger than life and beyond human comprehension, as remote to Job as Zeus on Olympus was to Odysseus. Quite naturally, Job grovels on the ground before THE LORD, "repenting in dust and ashes," even though God Himself had previously told Satan that Job was a blameless man who had nothing to repent.

Then, suddenly, God tells Job to pray for his friends. In that instant, we see the loving God in whose image we like to believe we have been created. God did not, as might have been expected from what went before, instruct Job to kowtow and worship Him. God did not, as Job had desired, explain to him the reasons for his suffering, nor did He tell him when or how it all might end. He simply told Job to pray for his friends.

Pray for your friends. Job might well have received that very same advice from a good friend, a minister, or the members of a support group. With that command, THE LORD becomes God. The power who planted the mountains on the earth and who placed the stars in the sky becomes the loving counselor concerned for Job and his friends, and who listens to their prayers. Whether or not Job's friends were beneficiaries of Job's prayer is irrelevant. *Job* was the real beneficiary of Job's prayer.

In *Prayer: Finding the Heart's True Home,* Richard Foster writes how, through our prayers, "God's loving friendship draws us *inward* into the transformation we need: changing us, molding us, forming us." But beyond that, Foster says that we are also called "*outward* into the ministry we need: healing the sick, suffering with the broken, interceding for the world" (emphasis in original). It was in just these ways that Job began to be transformed, to once again become whole.

That's why God told Job to pray for his friends and, through Job's example, has given the same guidance to every generation since, right down to our age. We are told to pray for others because in doing so we become better and stronger people ourselves. In rising above our problems, we begin to see new solutions for those problems, and to reach out for the help we need to solve them. And who knows, as we become better and stronger by praying for our friends we just might – like Job – forget about our grievances, stop complaining about how we have been victimized by circumstances we cannot control, and begin to do more of the things that earn success in worldly terms. Just like Job did.

Transforming Organizations

In *Jesus CEO: Using Ancient Wisdom for Visionary Leadership,* Laurie Beth Jones asks us to "imagine what kind of management this nation would have if CEOs spent as much time mulling and praying over their staffers' growth as they did over their budget reports." She goes on to say: "Leaders and managers often spend too much energy trying to make the numbers dance. Anyone can tell you that numbers don't dance. Only people do."

In recent years, a great deal has been written about servant leadership, including a number of books holding out Jesus as a role model of leadership through service and self-sacrifice. Praying for the people upon whom the success of your organization, and perhaps your own future career, depend is a natural extension of this concept.

Any organization in which leaders prayed for their employees would be much less likely to treat people as expendable cogs in a machine, or to push them into activities that are unethical or illegal. If the leaders at Enron and WorldCom, or more recently Wells Fargo and Boeing, had spent more time praying for their people, and the customers they served, and less time worrying about the numbers, they could have prevented the ethical failures that caused such unpleasant headlines.

And what if individual employees were to pray for their friends (coworkers)? What if, instead of hanging around the water-cooler gossiping about who was doing what to whom, people were to ask themselves and each other how they might best help and support who and whom, and silently pray for their success and welfare? Wouldn't such an organization be a more positive and productive place to work? Wouldn't we see fewer references in the management literature to bullying, incivility, disengagement, and burnout – and as a result do a better job of recruiting and retaining the best talent, serving and earning the loyalty of customers, and more effectively competing in the marketplace?

Transforming
the World

God told Job to pray for the small circle of his friends. Jesus expanded that circle when he said, "But I tell you: Love your enemies and pray for those who persecute you." Imagine how different our world would be if people truly took this command to heart. How much more harmonious and productive would our nation be if we demanded that standard of politicians and refused to vote for those who demonized their opponents and promoted hatred in pursuit of their own political agendas? The answer to the question posed on wristbands – WWJD, What Would Jesus Do? – might well be PFYF – Pray For Your Friends.

The answer to the question posed on wrist-bands – WWJD, What Would Jesus Do? – might well be PFYF – Pray For Your Friends.

My good friend and business school classmate Kien Pham and his family lost everything when the North Vietnamese Army rolled into Saigon (since renamed Ho Chi Minh City) in the final days of the Vietnam War. His father was sent away to prison, their home was confiscated, and the family was reduced to poverty. They finally escaped Vietnam in a boat with only the clothes on their backs. Kien arrived in the U.S. with no money and speaking no English but went on to become a modern-day Horatio Alger story. Following a successful career in business and government service, Kien established the Vietnam Education Foundation to help Vietnamese graduate students, including children of the men who had dispossessed his family after the war, study at America's top universities.

Today, Kien and his family live in Ho Chi Minh City where he devotes his considerable energies to helping to modernize that country's business and education infrastructures, and where he has become one of Vietnam's most respected business leaders and philanthropists. And he does not allow the fact that he has gone blind to be an excuse for not doing the work that he has been called to do. Like Job four millennia before him, Kien surmounted adversity by devoting himself to the service of others – to praying for his friends, including new friends who once were enemies. As was the case with Job, Kien's worldly success came *after* his commitment to serve others – his commitment to pray for his friends.

Transforming
Yourself

The late Norman Vincent Peale wrote that the second great commandment instructs us to love our neighbors *as ourselves*. He then asked why we so often forget those last two words (my wife says this might explain why some people treat their neighbors so badly). Praying for your friends sometimes begins with a prayer for yourself. It begins by praying that you have the moral strength and the inner peace to sincerely pray for others, and the courage and determination to make those prayers visible in your attitudes and behaviors. Praying for your friends softens your heart, which is often the first step to praying for yourself. The eight prayers I describe in the next section could transform your life the way they transformed the life of Job.

Part 2

THE 8 PRAYERS

OF JOB

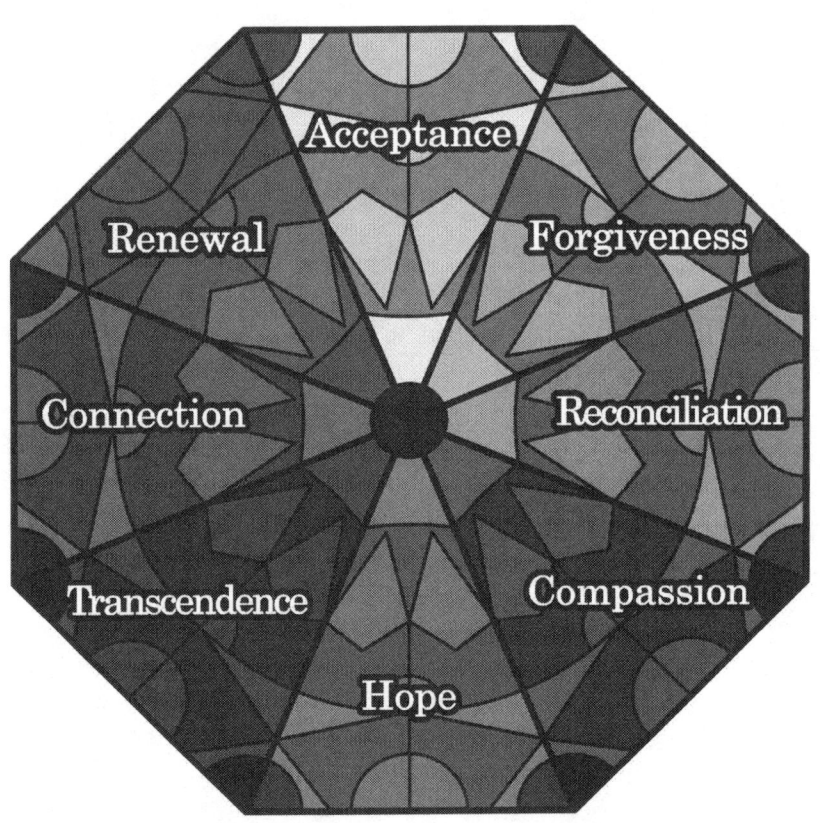

1.
A Prayer
for Acceptance

"Consider it pure joy, my brothers, whenever you face
trials of many kinds, because you know the testing of
your faith develops perseverance."

James 1:2

In her classic book *On Death and Dying*, Elisabeth
Kübler-Ross outlined the stages of the dying process
as including denial, anger, bargaining, depression,
and finally (hopefully!) culminating in acceptance.
Although in the story Job did not die for another
140 years, in the aftermath of Satan's assault he went
through each of these stages as if he were dying (and
indeed, he prayed for his own death). Upon hearing

the news that his ten children had been killed in a freak accident, he responded with the sort of nonchalance that is characteristic of denial (the Lord giveth and the Lord taketh away – oh well). After Satan ravaged his body with leprosy, Job became angry at God for allowing all those bad things to happen to him, good man that he was. Then he began to bargain that he simply be allowed to confront his tormentor so that he could demand answers. Ultimately, he was so depressed that he wished for his own death. Because of time compression that occurs in story-telling, Job appears to have experienced these emotions almost simultaneously. Only eventually, and only after having been confronted by God emerging from the whirlwind and instructing him to pray for his friends, did Job reach some semblance of acceptance.

Until Job could accept that, yes indeed, these bad things had happened to him, and that they would not un-happen, he would remain rooted in the past, playing the role of the victim. Self-perceived victims never prosper (which is why so many lottery "winners" end up bankrupt within a year or so – victims are still victims even after being given money they did not earn and which in their hearts they know they do not deserve). To be receptive to future blessings, Job had to free himself from the grip of past tragedies. He had to make the mental transition from "why me?" to "was me" and move on. To use one of my favorite metaphors, it's better to be a three-legged coyote than a four-legged fur coat. Job had to chew off the paw of the past before he could begin to envision a better future. To be receptive to future blessings, Job had to free himself from the grip of past tragedies.

To be receptive to future blessings, Job had to free himself from the grip of past tragedies.

For the person who is dying, acceptance might be an end-stage, but for the person who is just *passing through* the valley of the shadow, acceptance is usually a precondition for emerging from the shadows and ascending back into the light. Accepting the loss is almost always the first step toward creating meaning from an otherwise meaningless tragedy.

When God told Job to pray for his friends, He was telling him to accept the facts that a string of bad things had happened to him, and that his friends had been less than helpful or sympathetic. Job had to let go of that sad past. Only then would he open himself up to the blessings of the future. The human mind is capable of holding only one train of thought at a time. You cannot simultaneously be complaining about your own troubles and praying for the success and happiness of someone else. You cannot simultaneously see yourself as a victim of your past and as the creator of your future. "Pray for your friends" is a powerful prescription for acceptance and equanimity.

You cannot simultaneously be complaining about your own troubles and praying for the success and happiness of someone else. You cannot simultaneously see yourself as a victim of your past and as the creator of your future.

The late Father Michael Crosby wrote a biography of Solanus Casey titled *Thank God Ahead of Time.* That's a great philosophy for dealing with the tragedies and travesties of life. When I'm speaking about courage and perseverance, I often ask listeners to visualize the mnemonic TGAoT stenciled on the insides of their foreheads as a way of pre-programming their thinking to accept adversity and loss as a well-disguised blessing, not as a curse. Bad things do happen to good people; if you've prepared yourself ahead of time with the TGAoT commitment to face those bad things with courage and equanimity, the silver linings will become evident much more quickly.

I've spent many evenings with support groups and have often witnessed people discover blessings deeply hidden in such bad things as cancer, addiction or the loss of a loved one. I can't help but believe that in Job's day there were people who found well-disguised blessings even in leprosy, the disease which Satan had inflicted upon Job after having had his family and servants killed. For some, living in a leper colony might have been their first and only experience of true community.

But what about the murder of Job's children? No blessing could possibly be hidden in the deaths of young people. But even here, grieving parents have a choice to make: either they allow the death to be a meaningless tragedy, or they find a way to create meaning. When Candace Lightner's daughter was killed by a drunk driver, rather than take up permanent residence in the valley of the shadow of grief, she founded Mothers Against Drunk Driving (MADD). Her commitment to preventing other parents from experiencing the tragedy that had darkened her doorstep was a profoundly eloquent way of praying for friends she would never meet. It's been estimated that thanks to the work of MADD, more than 300,000 people are alive today who otherwise would have been killed by drunk drivers – all beneficiaries of a woman who transformed her own tragedy into a commitment to care about others.

When you pray for your friends, you transfer your gaze from looking inward to looking outward. Praying for others, and taking action on their behalf, rather than feeling sorry for yourself, is the first step to accepting the loss – the first step to chewing off the paw that has you stuck in the trap of the past and moving forward toward the blessings of the future.

When you pray for your friends, you transfer your gaze from looking inward to looking outward, from being stuck in a bitter past to moving toward a better future.

2.

A PRAYER
FOR FORGIVENESS

"Forgive us our trespasses, as we forgive
those who trespass against us."

The Lord's Prayer

When bad things happen, bad feelings can be created. Sometimes one of the greatest challenges of dealing with adversity is finding forgiveness. In many respects, the quality of our lives will be determined by the extent to which we are able to forgive – forgive ourselves, our parents, other people, and even God.

One time I'd been fired from a job in such a way as to create a lot of bad feelings and painful emotions. My anger was so toxic it was driving out every positive emotion and bubbled so close to the surface that it was making it almost impossible for me to effectively search for another job. I was living out the classic definition of a grudge: drinking poison in hopes of hurting someone else.

While this was going on, I told a friend that even though I knew this hateful grudge was darkening every corner of my life, its hold was too strong; I simply could not let it go. I couldn't fight it, and I couldn't run away from it. Even as I recognized my lesser self of ego suffocating my better self of soul, I could not chew off the paw and move on.

"The solution is simple," my friend told me. "You've got to pray for the success of the person who fired you."

I shook my head. "I can't do it. It's not in my heart to pray that prayer."

"That doesn't matter," my friend replied. "You just say the words. Say them every day, as if you mean them. Saying that prayer will break the ice. Keep at it, and eventually the ice will melt."

My friend was right. It didn't happen overnight, but gradually the grudge released its hold on me. In *The Spirituality of Imperfection,* Ernest Kurtz and Katherine Ketchum write that forgiveness is a miracle, because it's not something you can will upon yourself. It certainly felt like a miracle to me the day I realized that my prayer had been granted. I had no idea whether the man who'd fired me was successful. What I did know was that I genuinely *hoped* he was successful. I had forgiven him. He might not have cared a whit whether or not I'd forgiven him, but that didn't matter. For me, the peace I'd gained liberated me from the dead weight of an unchangeable past.

This miracle of forgiveness brought in its wake the blessing of clarity. As I began to see through the anger and hostility, several other things became clear to me. First, not only did I need to forgive, I also needed to ask for forgiveness. For my part, I had not handled the separation in a particularly graceful manner.

This miracle of forgiveness brought in its wake the blessing of clarity.

More important, with forgiveness came the realization that being fired really was the proverbial best thing that ever could have happened. The reason I'd been fired was that I was trying to pound the squiggly peg of me into the square hole of a career that was not the work I was put on this earth to do. Forgiveness, including forgiveness for myself, freed me to find a new path in life, a path with heart (to borrow the memorable phrase of Carlos Castaneda).

As I mentioned, I've spent many evenings with support groups. I'm always inspired by the sharing of hope and courage that is the one gift people who have experienced tragedy can give to each other. The one exception was an evening I spent with a support group for parents whose children had been murdered. Most of these crimes remained unsolved. I don't think I've ever seen so much hatred and latent violence in one place. It felt as if, had one of the murderers been dragged into that room, those angry parents would have beaten him to death right then and there. Had that happened, a month later they would all have felt immeasurably more miserable for having taken out their vengeance. And the one thing that had been defining their lives would now be gone; how can one hate a dead murderer?

One man remarked that neither he nor his wife had enjoyed a single a moment of peace in the years since their daughter's battered body had been found in the trunk of a car. His wife nodded in agreement. I wanted to ask them what their daughter would say if she could return to Earth for just one minute. Would she say: "Mom and Dad, I want to thank you for honoring my memory by allowing your lives to have been ruined by my death." Or would it more likely have been: "Please, Mom and Dad, let go of the anger and hatred that have turned your hearts to ice. I have long since forgiven the person who took my life. Can't you find it in your hearts to do the same? Not because he deserves to be forgiven, but because you need to forgive."

When God told Job to pray for his friends, I believe He was also telling him to forgive them. Though they were undoubtedly trying to be helpful, they had in effect been telling Job that it was all his own fault. In so many words, they said that because of his past deeds, Job was guilty of causing the deaths of his children and his servants. Had Job not been a terrible person who had done terrible things, they implied, God would never have allowed these bad things to have happened to him. Job was clearly angered by these accusations. By instructing Job to pray for his friends, the way my friend told me to pray for the man who'd fired me, God was also telling him to forgive them.

By instructing Job to pray for his friends God was also telling him to forgive them.

Mahatma Gandhi said that only the strong can forgive. The second prayer of Job calls upon us to have that strength. The quality of our lives, and the nature of the world that we pass on to our children, will be profoundly influenced by whether or not we have the courage and the strength to heed that call. As Dr. Edward M. Hallowell says in his book *Dare to Forgive*:

> The greatest challenge we humans now face is not scientific or technological or even economic. It is emotional... The real demon is the ignorance and fear that lead to the hatred that leads to the judgments that lead to the killings in wars. No one is free of it. All we can do is try to refuse to live under its rule. All we can do is try to forgive.

The way Job was called upon to forgive his friends by praying for them.

3.

A Prayer
for Reconciliation

"First go and be reconciled to your brother;
then come offer your gift."

Matthew 5:24

After telling Job to "curse God and die," his wife (who, unlike Job, perhaps somehow intuited that God had colluded with Satan in the murder of her children, and whose name we never learn) disappears from the story. Not once does Job mention her in his lamentations. Whether it's because his heart had been broken or because his soul had been turned to ice we cannot know, but it's hardly likely that her lack of support during his time of tribulation endeared her to him. Of course, his obvious absence of concern for her feelings could hardly have endeared him to her – they were, after all, also *her* children who were killed by Satan's mighty wind.

When Job grew his post-catastrophe family of seven new sons and three new daughters, was he still married to the same woman who had once told him to curse God and die, the mother of his first ten children whose name he never uttered while speaking to his friends? Did the two of them reconcile? We cannot know from the story itself, but we might make the inference that they stayed together from other biblical stories of aged patriarchs who sired children late in life.

According to my Webster's Unabridged Dictionary, there are multiple meanings of the word "reconciliation." It can mean resigning oneself to an undesired fate, though that's hopefully not how Job and his wife would have viewed the rest of their lives together. Reconciliation also means ending a quarrel or bringing previously estranged people together in harmony – as in repairing a damaged marriage. Most interesting of all, reconciliation can also mean re-consecration of something sacred that has been desecrated. It truly is a sacred event when a broken relationship is mended. But to make the necessary amends often requires courage, vulnerability, and a willingness to set aside pride and ego. Someone must go out on a limb to start the reconciliation process.

It truly is a sacred event when a broken relationship is mended. But to make the necessary amends often requires courage, vulnerability, and a willingness to set aside pride and ego.

We do not know if Job's wife vanished from his life, but if the story were being told in the world of today, chances are that would have been the case. It is commonly reported that more than half of all new marriages in the United States end up in divorce. And while there are certainly marriages where everyone involved is better off after the couple separates, and many beautiful second marriages follow upon the fracturing of ugly first marriages, you have to wonder what people are missing out on when they break up. There is something exquisite about an older couple who, after having passed over the mountains and through the valleys, after having loved and hated one another, and yet stuck together through it all, are now two old souls, as comfortable with each other as an old dog and an old cat cuddled together in front of the fireplace.

So how do couples reconcile after their relationship has been shaken to the foundation – as Job's relationship with his wife certainly must have been during their time of trials? I mean that both in the sense of coming back together and of restoring a sense of sacredness to their partnership. I doubt there is one simple answer (I certainly don't know it if there is), but I do know this: reconciliation is not a one-time event in a marriage or any other relationship. Rather, it is an ongoing commitment to make that relationship work, whatever the difficulties. (I once overheard a wise old man tell a young man who was about to be married that a good marriage is never a 50-50 proposition, it is always 80-20; sometimes you're the 80, and sometimes you're the 20.) And the best place to start the reconciliation process is to pray for each other.

> **Reconciliation is not a one-time event in a marriage or any other relationship. Rather, it is an ongoing commitment to make that relationship work, whatever the difficulties.**

As important as it is in our personal relationships, a commitment to reconciliation is even more vital when it comes to the relationships between peoples, and between nations. Whether our leaders choose to follow a policy of reconciliation or a policy of aggression has enormous implications for the path of international affairs – not to mention for the lives of people who, depending upon the choices made by those leaders, will either be flying on commercial airliners for business trips or boarding troop transports to go fight in a war.

A quick history lesson: At the end of World War I, the allied powers set out to permanently cripple Germany. They confiscated some of her most productive territories, disbanded her military forces, and imposed financial reparations that caused enormous suffering to the German people. The allies wanted revenge, not reconciliation. But in sowing the seeds of vengeance, they reaped the whirlwind of Adolf Hitler and World War II.

After the Second World War, the opposite approach was taken – reconciliation rather than revenge. In the immediate aftermath of the war more than 40 million displaced people were left homeless, violence and revenge killing were endemic, and there were real fears that civil wars could break out across the ravaged continent. But facing these challenges, the allies took a very different tack than that which was taken in 1919. With implementation of the Marshall

Plan beginning in 1947, massive resources were invested in rebuilding the German economy and nation. More recently, when Ronald Reagan stood at the Berlin Wall and told Mikhail Gorbachev to "tear down this wall," he had the courage to stand up to an enemy that had to be defeated, coupled with the wisdom to know that you don't win lasting victories by killing people, you win them by making peace. As a result of a commitment to reconciliation that has spanned two generations, today a united Germany is a member in good standing of the world community.

In *The Lord of the Rings,* J.R.R. Tolkien had Gandalf the wizard say that "the hands of a king are the hands of a healer." Our times cry out for leaders who are committed to healing and reconciliation, and to closing the gaps that separate and segregate us from one another. We need leaders who inspire us to come together in a spirit of mutuality – we're all in this together – and to work toward the common good. No nation can afford the long-lasting damage caused by rulers who govern by stoking the emotionally caustic fires of hatred and fear.

Our times cry out for leaders who are committed to healing and reconciliation, and to

closing the gaps that separate and segregate us from one another.

In his often-quoted second inaugural address, Abraham Lincoln spoke of binding the nation's wounds "with malice toward none [and] with charity for all." He knew that a spirit of reconciliation was the only way to "achieve and cherish a just and lasting peace among ourselves and with all nations." In his first inaugural address, Lincoln had called upon people to heed "the nature of our better angels." And what better way to call upon those better angels than to pray for our friends – including those who once were enemies?

4.

A PRAYER
FOR COMPASSION

*"Seek justice, encourage the oppressed. Defend the
cause of the fatherless, plead the case of the widow."*

Isaiah 1:17

When God told Job to pray for his friends, He was instructing him to return their hardheartedness with compassion. Without ever knowing the true facts, they had jumped to the conclusion that Job must have been a bad person because of the bad things that had happened to him. "Far be it from God to do evil, for the Almighty to do wrong," proclaimed Job's young friend Elihu. "He repays a man for what he has done; he brings upon him what his conduct deserves." Not only was Job a sinner, Elihu continued, but he was also a rebel who in proclaiming his innocence was speaking out against God.

Why, Job might well have wondered, should he pray for the "miserable comforters" his friends had been. His only request to them had been to "have pity on me, my friends, have pity." Instead of pitying him, they hounded him with accusations of evilness and wrongdoing. Instead of sympathizing with his plight, they blamed him for the tragedies that had befallen his life. Why, indeed, should he pray for them?

Why? Perhaps God saw developing in Job the same hard-heartedness that his friends had showed toward him. After recounting all the things he had done for others ("I was like one who comforts mourners"), Job now becomes harsh and judgmental toward his friends, these men "whose fathers I would have disdained to put with my sheepdogs." From once having been a man who "rescued the poor who cried for help, and the fatherless who had none to assist him," Job was now becoming bitter and self-centered: "surely no one lays a hand on a broken man when he cries out for help in his distress."

One of the chief qualities of being human is the capacity for compassion. We revere Mother Teresa for the depth of compassion she gave to those taken into her care; we revile Nazi concentration camp guards for the absolute absence of compassion they showed toward the people they tormented. We think of Mother Teresa as being superhuman, and of those concentration camp guards as being less than human in every sense of that word that really matters.

One of the chief qualities of being human is the capacity for compassion.

Unfortunately, as Stephen Trzeciak and Anthony Mozzarelli document in their book *Compassionomics,* "There is a worldwide compassion crisis at the moment. Right now. And it matters." They say that "forty seconds of compassion is all you need to make a meaningful difference for a patient," and that what has become known as compassion fatigue is often caused by a failure to make time for these forty seconds. This failure of compassion is in turn a significant contributor to the plague of burnout in healthcare and in many other industries.

If you are a parent and have closely read Job's speech, I'll bet you were struck by this fact as I was: not once in his long lament did Job ever express sorrow for the loss of his ten children. Not once. His entire dialogue centered on himself. *Why me? How could God have let this happen to me? Me, me, me.*

When bad things happen, there is a tendency to sink into the swamp of solipsism, to feel that we are at the center of a collapsing universe, and that nothing else matters. Job himself says this of a man who has been flattened by catastrophe: "If his sons are honored, he does not know it; if they are brought low, he does not see it. He feels but the pain of his own body and mourns only for himself." Job's sons were killed by Satan's evil wind but Job could not see it; he could only feel the pain of his own body.

When bad things happen, there is a tendency to sink into the swamp of solipsism, to feel that we are at the center of a collapsing universe, and that nothing else matters.

Job asked his friends to have compassion for him; instead God demanded that Job have compassion for his friends.

When God told Job to pray for his friends, it was an instruction for future generations to act with compassion, but I believe it was something more: God was warning us against victim-blame, a mindset that almost always precedes compassionless attitudes and behaviors. Job's friends lacked compassion for his travails because they assumed he was to blame, that since bad things had happened to him he must have been a bad person to deserve them. It was perhaps the first description in recorded history of the psychology of blaming the victim, but certainly not the last. We hear echoes of Job's friends down to our own day, for example when politicians justify miserly social support services by implicitly blaming poor people for their poverty, or the way stressed-out emergency room doctors and nurses can complain about "frequent fliers" who keep showing up in their emergency rooms because they have nowhere else to go.

There is a fascinating postscript to Job's story. We are told that after his fortunes were restored, Job had seven more sons and three more daughters. Only the daughters are named – Jememiah, Keziah, and Keren-Happuch. Not only that, we are told that Job granted them an inheritance along with their broth-ers. The fact that the author chose to highlight Job's treatment of his daughters tells us how extraordinary it must have been at the time.

The same Job who never even mentions the deaths of his first children breaks tradition by granting an inheritance to his daughters as well as to his sons. This must reflect the way his heart was softened by compassion. The more Job prayed for his friends, the more he saw the human beings underneath the superficiality of appearances. He saw his children as human souls, not just boys or girls. In the well-known formulation of Martin Buber, before he learned to pray for his friends Job lived in the paradigm of I-It. He was the center of his own little universe, and his children were among the possessions that orbited around him. At some point after he began praying for his friends, Job moved toward living in Buber's I-Thou paradigm. In Job's new eyes, his daughters were just as human, just as deserving, as his sons.

5.

A Prayer
for Hope

"Hope deferred makes the heart sick,
but a longing fulfilled is a tree of life."

Proverbs 13:12

When God told Job to pray for his friends, he was effectively changing the subject. Job wanted answers, to know why he was being made to suffer. God was not going to give Job those answers. But God also knew that Job didn't need answers – what he needed more than anything was hope. After the devastating losses he had suffered, Job had no hope for a better future. Indeed, all he wanted from the future was to not be there when it arrived. It is but a short step from being hopeless to being helpless, and Job was hopeless. To lose hope is to risk losing everything.

For people who are trudging through the valley of the shadow, hope might be the only thing that keeps them planting one foot in front of the other, when it would be so easy, and so tempting, to just give up and quit. For the wife of the abusive alcoholic, for the man who's been told that his cancer is inoperable, for the couple whose child has been sent to prison, hope might be all there is.

For people who are trudging through the valley of the shadow, hope might be the only thing that keeps them planting one foot in front of the other, when it would be so easy, and so tempting, to just give up and quit.

In the world of business it is often said that hope is not a strategy. True enough, but it is also true that without hope even the most brilliant strategy is doomed. One of the leader's paramount obligations is to instill hope, if for no other reason than that hope is sometimes the only thing that will salvage a failed strategy or save the company from the consequences of that failure.

In *Team of Rivals: The Political Genius of Abraham Lincoln,* Doris Kearns Goodwin writes of Abraham Lincoln's response to the Union Army's devastating loss at the battle of Chancellorsville in May of 1863: "As he had done so many times before, Lincoln withstood the storm of defeat by replacing anguish over an unchangeable past with hope in an uncharted future." Before leaders can instill hope in others, they must nurture and sustain their own hope.

When I'm speaking with groups about the power of vision, I will occasionally suggest that they begin a practice of writing their own daily horoscope. I call it a Youroscope. "It's a Youroscope," I'll say, "not a to-do list, so be extravagant. Shoot for the moon. Wish for anything you want, from out of the blue, just so long as your wish is authentic. Then believe it will happen." What I'm doing with this seemingly silly exercise is encouraging people to dream bigger dreams, and then to hope for their fulfillment, knowing that hope is an essential precursor to effective action. People are much more likely to act if they are hopeful of success than if they expect to be disappointed.

People are much more likely to act if they are hopeful of success than if they expect to be disappointed.

Several months after having conducted a leadership retreat in which I prescribed this daily personal horoscope exercise, I received an e-mail from a participant who had written in her Youroscope that a relationship with a long-estranged friend would be restored. That's all she did – express in writing the hope that a burned-down bridge would be rebuilt. Not long after she wrote in her Youroscope, this woman got a phone call from the estranged friend inviting her out to lunch. It was, she said, a miracle.

I love the saying that coincidence is simply God's way of remaining anonymous. And I hear stories like this often enough to believe that it's more than random chance or dumb luck; such miracles really do happen. So while I don't really believe that God will physically intervene in the world to cure one person's cancer, or to stop a speeding car from running over a pedestrian, I do believe there is something divine, something miraculous about the power of hope.

There's another beautiful thing about hope. You don't have to justify it. If I tell you I'm *optimistic* that world peace is just around the corner, you could quite reasonably ask me for the grounds upon which I would make such a statement (and given what's going on in the world today, they would be flimsy grounds indeed). But if I say that I *hope* world peace is just around the corner, I don't need any reason for that hope – I just hope. As Saint Paul famously commented in his first letter to the Corinthians, when combined with faith and love, hope is a powerful force indeed.

Finally, a word about false hope: there's no such thing. All hope is genuine, real, and true, whether or not it turns out to have been predictive. One of the worst things you can do to another person is take away their hope. Every doctor worth his or her diploma knows this; they deliberately foster hope in their patients, knowing that it has a powerful curative impact. The technical term for this is the placebo effect. It is grounded on the truth that there is power in hope (and powerlessness in hopelessness).

In *Velvet Elvis: Repainting the Christian Faith*, Rob Bell writes: "Ultimately our gift to the world around us is hope. Not blind hope that pretends everything is fine and refuses to acknowledge how things are. But the kind of hope that comes from staring pain and suffering right in the eyes and refusing to believe that this is all there is. It is what we all need – hope that comes not from going around suffering but from going through it." My novel *The Healing Tree* includes this poem:

The Hope Diamond

The most precious diamond in the world
cannot be purchased, it can only be accepted.

The most precious diamond in the world cannot
be seen, it can only be felt.

The most precious diamond in the world cannot
be worn around your neck, it can only be kept
safe in your heart.

The most precious diamond in the world cannot
be taken away, it can only be given away.

The most precious diamond in the world is free for
the asking, and you can have as many as you ask for.

The most precious diamond in the world is stronger
than iron, but is more fragile than a dream.

The most precious diamond in the world is always genuine,
because there's no such thing as false hope.

There truly is no such thing as false hope. If you lose hope it usually just means that you are not looking far enough ahead. When you pray for your friends, you are giving away Hope Diamonds; you are encouraging people with the hope they need to "stare pain and suffering right in the eyes." And the more Hope Diamonds you give away, the more of them you are likely to receive in return.

If you lose hope it usually just means that you are not looking far enough ahead.

6.

A Prayer
for Transcendence

*"And what does the Lord require of you? To act justly
and to love mercy and to walk humbly with your God."*

Micah 6:8

Many years ago, in the days when the AIDS epidemic first exploded upon the national consciousness, I volunteered at a shelter for homeless people who had AIDS, which in those days meant that they would all soon die. During my tenure, the shelter was ruled with a gentle touch by a woman I'll call Sylvia. In her early fifties, she herself was dying of the disease. She had contracted AIDS by injecting herself with a contaminated needle. At that time, she had less than a year to live.

I was "between jobs" at the time and had been wallowing around in the swamp of self-pity for much too long. If nothing else, volunteering got me out of the house. I had worked myself into a pretty serious double bind, which is the term psychologists use to describe a self-inflicted lose-lose predicament. My ego was unwilling to settle for anything less than the high-pay, high-status career track I'd been on, but my soul was throwing up every emotional barrier imaginable to prevent me from searching for another job that would force me to continue pretending to be someone different than the person I was put on this earth to become. When I walked through the doors of what I came to know as Sylvia's House, I forgot about the inner battle between ego and soul as I tackled whatever menial task she assigned me for my shift.

One day we were talking and I asked her a question. It was a question I've asked many people since. The answer is almost always the same. I asked her, if she could go back and undo the act of sticking that infected needle into her arm and thus never had contracted AIDS, but the price would be that she'd be the person she would have been had it never happened, would she do it?

She didn't hesitate for one second. "No way," she replied. "I'd love to be cured, but I wouldn't trade one minute of my life with AIDS for another ten years of my life as the party girl." She went on to tell me how, for the first time, she had real friends, not just drinking buddies; about how glorious it was to wake up in the morning and see the sunrise through clear eyes, unclouded by the hangover of unremembered activities from the night before; and above all, that precisely because of AIDS she now understood what Jesus meant when He'd said that you must lose your life in order to gain it. The real Sylvia had only been able to emerge when Party Girl Sylvia died. The joy she now felt in helping her friends far exceeded any rush she'd ever experienced from booze or drugs.

"You know why they call it a trip?" she asked me one day, referring to the drug-induced high. "They call it a trip because you're running away – running away from yourself. When my body started to fall apart, I had to stop running. And when I stopped running, I finally found the real me. And you know what? I really like the real me."

In *The Heart of Christianity,* Marcus J. Borg writes about how our culture is filled with messages that promote appearance, achievement, and affluence. As we obsess about how we stack up on these measures, he says, "we fall farther into the world of separation and alienation, comparison and judgment." This tendency can be especially harmful during times of adversity. When bad things happen, we often compound the tragedy by our emotional reaction to it. Instead of straightforwardly dealing with the problem, we worry about what other people might think of us (appearance), how it might affect our careers (achievement), and what it's going to cost us (affluence). The call to pray for your friends is also a call to transcend superficial self-interest by reaching out to others.

When bad things happen, we often compound the tragedy by our emotional reaction to it.

When God told Job to pray for his friends, I think He was directing him to rise above his ego and connect with his soul. Ego is inner-directed and self-centered; soul is outer-directed and other-centered. Ego wants status and possessions; soul wants loving relationships and spiritual peace. Ego counts success in terms of income; soul counts success in terms of outgo. Ego wants to have friends; soul wants to be a friend. Ego is always running away from something or running after something; soul wants to stop and appreciate that heaven is right here, right now. A prayer for friends is ultimately a prayer for transcendence.

In *The Power of Myth* Joseph Campbell wrote: "When we stop thinking primarily about ourselves and our own self-preservation we undergo a truly heroic transformation of consciousness." We can imagine that Job must have experienced that heroic transformation himself. Can't you just visualize Job as an old man: at peace with himself, at peace with the world, and at peace with God as he watched his children grow to be strong adults and reveled at the sight of grandchildren and great-grandchildren down to the fourth generation playing at his feet? Transcending the tragedies of his past was an essential catalyst for the regeneration that created a beautiful new future.

7.

A Prayer
for Connection

*"Two are better than one, because they have a good
return for their work: If one falls down,
his friend can help him up."*

Ecclesiastes 3: 9-10

The first tragedy that strikes a person often brings a secondary tragedy in its wake: at a time when we most need the strength of human connection, we feel most isolated. The middle-aged man who's been laid off from his job loses more than just a job, or even his sense of identity – he loses his connection with a place and people that have given his life purpose and meaning. The woman sitting by the phone waiting to learn whether the lump in her breast is benign or malignant is profoundly alone, even if the room is full of concerned people.

When God told Job to pray for his friends, He was trying to push him out of his shell, to rebuild the relationships that his suffering had sundered. In the course of the story, Job saw the men who had once been his friends become "miserable comforters" who accused him of crimes he did not commit, and of a past wickedness that violated his sense of righteousness. Though they might have had the best of intentions, they were not acting like friends. In reaction, Job drew back and isolated himself. And his isolation and alienation from former friends intensified his suffering.

God knew that before Job could possibly appreciate any future blessings that might come to him, he had to first reconnect with humanity. To build and manage his new estate (twice what he had before!) would require the help of many people. To raise his new family (ten children!) would require patching the hole in his soul, and once again touching others and allowing himself to be touched by them in return.

God knew that before Job could possibly appreciate any future blessings that might come to him, he had to first reconnect with humanity.

I'll never forget speaking with a nurse who had come to America from the Philippines. "In my village," she told me, "the people are poor. But at the end of our workday, we gather in the square. Somebody brings out a transistor radio, and we dance and sing and laugh. In your country, people go home after work and close their doors so that no one will disturb their television. We are poor in things, but yours is the greater poverty."

Recent studies have shown that today we are more socially isolated, and that we have fewer friends, than any previous generation. We have, to quote the title of Robert D. Putnam's book on the loss, and hoped-for renewal, of the American spirit of community, grown accustomed to "bowling alone." In every airport, you'll see many more people connected to their laptops and cell phones than you will conversing with the person sitting in the seat next to them. In essence, they are all "bowling alone."

In Alcoholics Anonymous, there is a principle known as "mutuality." When recovering alcoholics reach out to other alcoholics, they're not solely trying to help that other person stay sober; they are also acknowledging that *they need to help* that other person stay sober in order to remain sober themselves. They are part of a mutually-dependent dyad. To offer help without also acknowledging that you need help runs the risk of being condescending, paternalistic, and judgmental. For the struggling alcoholic, help like this can be worse than no help at all. It is the help of "miserable comforters" who, consciously or not, seem to be blaming you for your misfortune. Whether or not the alcoholic deserves such blame, it's often the last thing they need to hear. They've already got plenty of self-blame and self-loathing. They don't need extra blame and loathing dumped on top of it by the miserable comforters in their lives.

Mutuality is the key to connection, it is the essence of teamwork, and it lies at the very heart of effective leadership. In his Pulitzer Prize-winning book *Leadership*, James MacGregor Burns described "transforming leadership" as a bilateral relationship between leader and followers in which *both* are transformed as a result of the interaction. In other words, transforming leadership is a relationship of mutuality – and mutuality requires a willingness to bring down the mental and emotional barriers that prevent connection.

Mutuality is the key to connection, it is the essence of teamwork, and it lies at the very heart of effective leadership.

One reason support groups can be so profoundly life-changing is that, by keeping the focus on a common and shared adversity, they strip away superficiality and pretense, making possible human connection at a deeper level. When the big-shot CEO who is a tyrannical egomaniac in the office finally summons the courage to stand in front of a room full of strangers and say, "I'm Harold and I'm an alcoholic," he's putting himself at the same level as the fellow drunk who will be walking over to the soup kitchen after the meeting. Only by admitting his weakness could this man accept in his heart the graceful truth that we are all children of the same God (the beautiful phrase coined by Mother Teresa in her book *A Simple Path*). And only by accepting that truth can we hope to connect with others at a deeper level.

Mutuality is based upon empathy and the companion understanding that not only are we all children of the same God, we are also all riders who happen to be at different points on the same roller coaster. The hectoring of Job's friends was devoid of empathy; as a result, rather than connecting with Job, they pushed him even farther away. When God tells us to pray for our friends, He is instructing us to listen rather than preach, to understand before we seek to be understood, and to connect with empathy rather than to pass judgment.

Mutuality is based upon empathy and the companion understanding that not only are we all children of the same God, we are also all riders who happen to be at different points on the same roller coaster.

8.

A PRAYER
FOR RENEWAL

"The Lord is my Shepherd; I shall not want.
He maketh me to lie down in green pastures:
He leadeth me beside the still waters.
He restoreth my soul"

23rd Psalm

"After Job had prayed for his friends, the Lord made him prosperous again and gave him twice as much as he had before." When I first read that passage in the Book of Job, I was reminded of the story about the woman who had toiled for years to cultivate the most beautiful garden in her land. One day a stranger passed by and stopped to marvel at the breathtaking splendor of her creation. "My goodness," he said to her, "the Lord has certainly blessed you with a magnificent garden." She nodded thoughtfully then replied, "Yes indeed, but you should have seen what it looked like when the Lord had it all to Himself."

When God told Job to pray for his friends, He effectively changed the subject, refocusing Job's attention away from the past that could not be changed and toward the future where action was within his power. After Job lost his family and his health, all the treasure in the world would not have rescued him from the swamp of self-pity and despair. Something else had to occur between Job's prayer for his friends and the recovery of his health and subsequent good fortune. He would need the courage to dream again, to risk again, and to work again. Job needed renewal, to be reborn in the very best sense of the word.

After Job lost his family and his health, all the treasure in the world would not have rescued him from the swamp of self-pity and despair. He would need the courage to dream again, to risk again, and to work again.

Certainly, Job was no stranger to risk and hard work. You don't build the sort of estate Job had before his run-in with Satan without a willingness to take risks and without lots of hard work. The portrait of Job before the predations of Satan is of a man who is enthusiastic, self-assured, and capable. He had seven sons and three daughters, thousands of sheep, camels, and assorted other beasts, and many servants. "He was," we are told, "the greatest man among all the people of the East."

With all the labors behind him, and his children growing into roles of responsibility, Job must also have been at a point in life when men naturally look forward to slowing down, to passing along the burdens of labor and management to their offspring, and to enjoying their golden years in the company of a growing horde of grandchildren. Virtually over-night, Job was robbed of these dreams. Everything had been taken from him, and taken in the most brutal manner imaginable. All that he had worked for his entire life – family, flocks, estate, health – was gone. He was broken, body and soul.

Job was devastated. "Why did I not perish at birth," he wails, "and die as I came from the womb?" His worst nightmares have become his daytime reality. He longs for death that will not come. "I have no peace, no quietness; I have no rest, but only turmoil." Had the setting been a modern city, you could picture Job standing on the ledge of a tall building uttering his last words before doing a swan dive onto the pavement far below.

Yet Job did not end it all. He somehow found the strength and the courage to pick up the few remaining pieces of his life and start all over again. The tragedies visited upon Job by Satan did not kill him, they made him stronger. We're told that Job had seven more sons and three more daughters, that his herds and flocks grew to twice what they had been before the disasters, and that he lived another 140 years to watch his children and four generations of grandchildren grow up in his household.

Where did Job – old, tired, broken man that he was – find the courage and the energy to rise phoenix-like from the dust and ashes and rebuild his life, and rebuild it in splendor far surpassing what he had before? The Bible tells us that after he prayed for his friends God made him prosperous again. But in truth, God does not "make you prosperous." God did not give Job a winning ticket to the Chaldean lottery. For a man like Job, being given wealth without having had to work for it, without having earned it, would have been insulting and toxic to his soul. A man like Job needed to work hard, needed to earn his wealth, not to have it handed to him on a silver platter as he reclined on the cushions.

What God *did* do was restore Job's spirit, give him back the courage, the energy, and the drive to take the risks and do the work which gave his life a sense of purpose and meaning. The Good Shepherd restored Job's soul.

Many scholars believe that the happy ending in which Job was granted a new family, incredible wealth, and unimaginably long life was a late addition appended to the original story. But if that's true, it in no way diminishes the *real* happy ending – that Job overcame the tragedies and found a renewed will to live, to work, to love, and to create. The real happy ending was not to be measured in material things, but in Job's renewed spirit. Lacking that renewal, all the wealth of Midas would have meant little. Job's renewal was the miraculous outcome of praying for his friends.

Conclusion

I will turn every complaint into either a blessing
or a constructive suggestion.

The Pickle Pledge

There is no inherent blessing in the loss of a child. It must be created through constructive action. I'll never forget an evening spent with members of a chapter of Compassionate Friends, a support group for parents who have lost a child, that most incomprehensible and inconsolable of tragedies. As we went around the room, each parent shared some part of their story: how their child had died, a favorite memory of their time together, a lesson they had learned, something they were doing to honor that child's memory. As I listened, it occurred to me that we humans have a desperate need to share our stories with each other. Especially the stories that break our hearts.

This sharing of stories is a reflection of our need to somehow connect with other human beings. Did you see the movie *Cast Away* with Tom Hanks? The character he played was marooned on a desert island with only a volleyball to keep him company. By movie's end Wilson the volleyball had become his debate partner, his best friend, his soulmate. The need for human-to-human connection is so deeply ingrained in our genes that we will manufacture another person out of thin air (or out of a volleyball) if the real thing is not available.

To pray for your friends is to reach out and make that human connection. "Pray for your friends" is God's invitation to share your story with others. It is God's invitation to rise above pettiness, selfishness, and self-centeredness, and to participate more fully in the family that we make up, we who are all children of the same God. It is a directive to forgive those who have hurt you, and to reconcile relationships that have been torn apart. It is a commandment to love your neighbor, and then to reach out with compassion and with empathy to people in other neighborhoods.

Pray for your friends. Then expand that circle of friendship by praying for those who could be (or should be) your friends. Work on creating a broader community by being the sort of servant leader who brings down silo walls and brings people together. When I try to read between the lines of the Book of Job – when I try as a mere mortal to read the mind of God – this is, I believe, the central message: Whatever has happened to you, rise above and reach out. It is also one of the central messages of the Bible. It is a natural extension of the Golden Rule, which in one form or another is central to each of the world's great cultural and religious traditions: pray for your friends as you would have your friends pray for you.

My favorite Bible passage is Mark 9:23 – all things are possible for one who believes. But if you read that story closely, it's not about belief at all. It's about love. In the story, a man's son had recurring fits and kept throwing himself into the fire. The father asked Jesus's disciples to help but they were unable to do so. So the father turned to Jesus. Jesus asked the man if he believed, saying that all things are possible for one who believes. "I believe," he exclaimed. "Help me overcome my unbelief." And the man's son was healed. Note carefully: Jesus was not demanding a specific belief of the man as prepayment for the miracle he desired. Had Jesus instructed him to sacrifice a goat to the almighty Zeus, the father would have done it out of love for his son. And Jesus still would have healed the son out of love for the father.

When the disciples were unable to help the man's son it was not because they lacked belief – it was because they lacked compassion. Jesus told them that the boy's affliction could be cured only by prayer. They were trying to make a miracle happen, not praying that a heartsick man get back his son. Jesus was praying for a friend – the miracle was a result of his love. If we would stop striving so hard for our own success and our own happiness and devote more of our energy to helping others achieve success and happiness – if we were to pray for our friends – perhaps we would indeed find that all things are possible.

THE END

Made in the USA
Columbia, SC
07 February 2022

55210821R00064